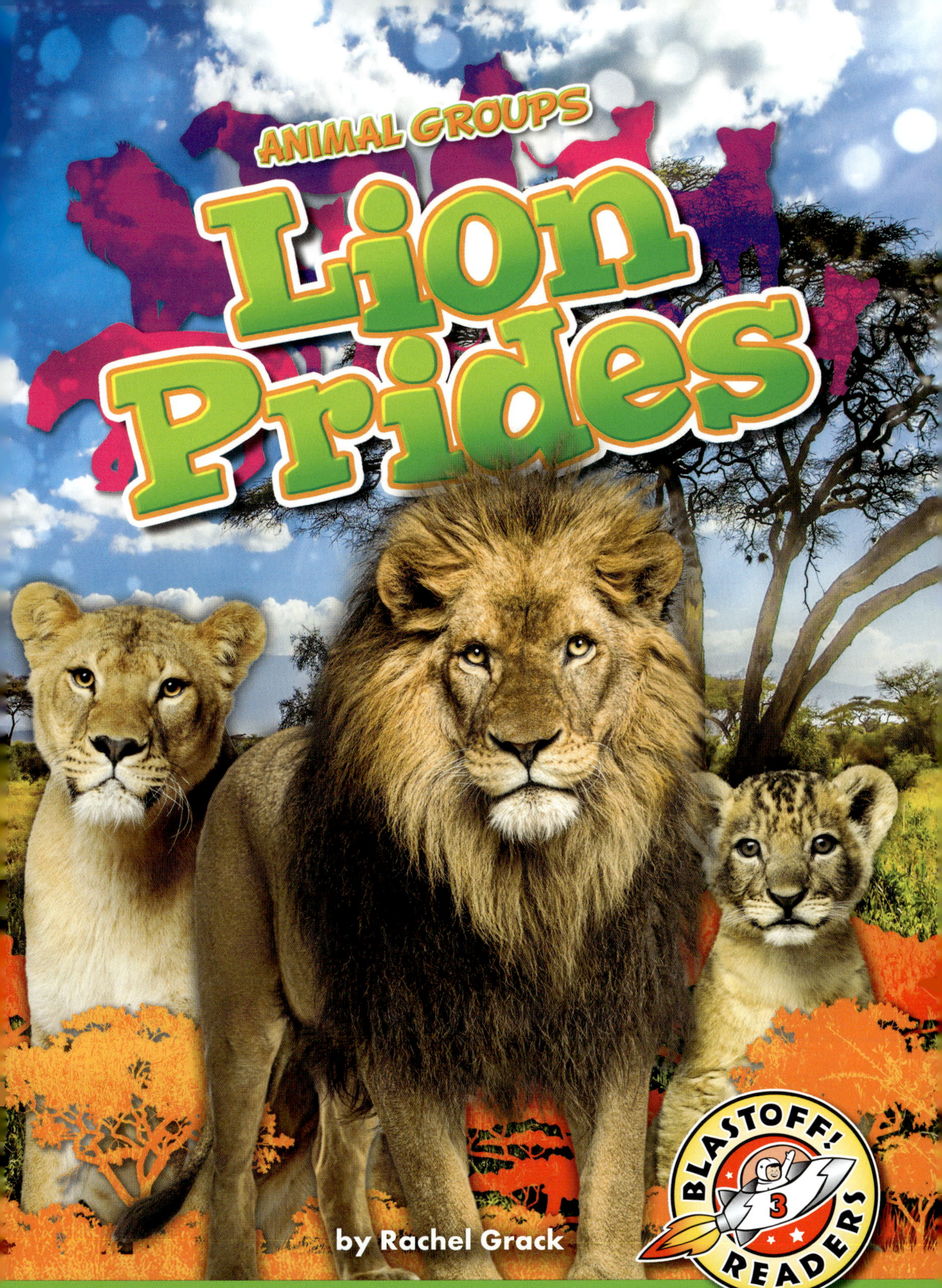

ANIMAL GROUPS

Lion Prides

by Rachel Grack

BELLWETHER MEDIA • MINNEAPOLIS, MN

Blastoff! Readers are carefully developed by literacy experts to build reading stamina and move students toward fluency by combining standards-based content with developmentally appropriate text.

Level 1 provides the most support through repetition of high-frequency words, light text, predictable sentence patterns, and strong visual support.

Level 2 offers early readers a bit more challenge through varied sentences, increased text load, and text-supportive special features.

Level 3 advances early-fluent readers toward fluency through increased text load, less reliance on photos, advancing concepts, longer sentences, and more complex special features.

★ Blastoff! Universe

Reading Level

Blastoff! Beginners — Grade K

Blastoff! Readers — Grades 1–3

Blastoff! Discovery — Grade 4

This edition first published in 2026 by Bellwether Media, Inc.

Library of Congress Cataloging-in-Publication Data

LC record for Lion Prides available at: https://lccn.loc.gov/2025018609

Editor: Suzane Nguyen Designer: Brittany McIntosh

Printed in the United States of America, North Mankato, MN.

Table of Contents

Lions are large and powerful wild cats. They once lived in Africa, Asia, and Europe.

Today, they mainly live on **savannas** in Africa. One **subspecies** remains in northwest India.

Pride Roles

Lions live together in **prides**. Some prides are small. Others have more than 40 lions.

Prides have mostly female lions. There are usually one to three males in a pride.

Prides share close **bonds**. Many members are family.

Male and female lions have different roles. Males guard the pride and **territory**. Females hunt for food and raise **cubs**.

Lions in a pride grunt and puff to greet one another. Sometimes they roar to **communicate**.

Communication

grunt and puff

greet one another

roar

call the pride together and keep other prides away

meow and purr

bond with cubs

Males roar to call the pride together. Roars also keep other prides away. Females meow and purr to bond with cubs.

Hunting Together

Female lions hunt for the pride. Sometimes males will help. Lions hunt wildebeests, zebras, and buffalo.

Lions **stalk** their **prey**. Then, they work together to take an animal down.

Lion Diet

wildebeests

zebras

buffalo

Female lions split into two groups. One group separates the prey from its **herd**. The other group waits to attack.

Male lions eat before females. Cubs eat last.

Working Together

1

female lions stalk prey

2

one group of lions separates the prey

3

the other group waits to attack

4

the pride eats

Lions are **apex predators**. Their size and strength scare other animals away.

Hyenas and cheetahs sometimes hunt lion cubs. Lions use their sharp teeth and claws to protect their young.

Caring for Cubs

Female lions have **litters** of two to four cubs. They hide their newborn cubs. This keeps the cubs safe.

Cubs join the pride when they grow stronger. The pride then helps raise the cubs.

Females stay with the pride as adults. Males leave the pride at about three years old.

Males wander alone until they find another pride. They must fight and win to join a new pride!

Glossary

apex predators—animals at the top of the food chain that are not preyed upon by other animals

bonds—strong attachments

communicate—to share thoughts and feelings using sounds, faces, actions

cubs—baby lions

herd—a group of animals that lives and travels together

litters—groups of animals born at the same time to one mother

prey—animals that are hunted by other animals for food

prides—groups of lions

savannas—flat grasslands with few trees

stalk—to quietly sneak up on

subspecies—groups of one type of animal that live in different parts of the world

territory—the land area where animals live

To Learn More

AT THE LIBRARY

Kenney, Karen Latchana. *Lion Prides*. Minneapolis, Minn.: Jump!, 2020.

Riggs, Kate. *Lions*. Mankato, Minn.: Creative Education and Creative Paperbacks, 2025.

Scheffer, Janie. *African Lions*. Minneapolis, Minn.: Bellwether Media, 2025.

ON THE WEB

FACTSURFER

Factsurfer.com gives you a safe, fun way to find more information.

1. Go to www.factsurfer.com.
2. Enter "lion prides" into the search box and click .
3. Select your book cover to see a list of related content.

Index

The images in this book are reproduced through the courtesy of: Eric Isselee, front cover (left lion, middle lion, right lion), pp. 3, 23; kavram, front cover (background); Maggy Meyer, p. 4; Images of Africa Photobank/ Alamy Stock Photo, p. 6; Dagmara Ksandrova, p. 7; Arturo de Frias, p. 8; Ozkan Ozmen, p. 9; 400tmax, pp. 10-11; Andrea Chiozzi, p. 11; Alta Oosthuizen, p. 12; Patrick Messier, pp. 12-13; Nick Dale Photo, p. 13 (wildebeests); U. Eisenlohr, p. 13 (zebras); Photography Phor Phun, p. 13 (buffalo); Amitrane, p. 14; Rudi Hulshof, p. 15 (step 1); mauritius images GmbH/ Alamy Stock Photo, p. 15 (step 2); Jez Bennett/ Alamy Stock Photo, p. 15 (step 3); steve bushman, p. 15 (step 4); Tony Campbell, p. 16; MintImages, p. 17; L Galbraith, p. 18; kjekol, p. 19; Reto Buehler, p. 20; Santiago Vigo, pp. 20-21.